REALLY WILD LIFE!

PATHFINDER EDITION

By Robyn Raymer and Dan Pine

CONTENTS

REALLY WILD LIFE!

By Robyn Raymer and Dan Pine

Western tarsier

Wallace's flying frog

Where can you find bearded pigs, pygmy elephants, and flying snakes? In one of the wildest places on Earth: Borneo.

Rhinoceros hornbill

Mattias Klum inches along the forest floor on his belly. Right in front of him, an enormous king cobra raises its head and flares its hood. It sways and eyes Klum.

The world's longest poisonous snake opens its mouth. It hisses and growls like an angry dog. The snake's tongue hangs out like a necktie.

Klum slowly stands up and backs away. In a flash, the snake slips back into Borneo's thick rain forest and is gone. For Klum, this rare glimpse of a wild king cobra is what Borneo is all about.

The Swedish photographer first came to the island in Southeast Asia 24 years ago. "I dreamed Borneo would be extraordinary in all ways," Klum says. "And it was true."

Rich Rain Forest

Klum found lush rain forests, soggy swamps, and rocky mountains. In some places, treetops brushed the clouds. He spotted hairy orangutans swinging from branch to branch. Birds chattered and insects hummed. Klum came face-to-face with some of the wildest creatures in the world. He saw flying snakes, bearded pigs, pygmy elephants, and more.

Klum had discovered one of the most **biodiverse** places on Earth. Nearly 1,500 kinds of animals live on Borneo, and that's not counting the bugs. Scientists found 1,000 different species of insects in just one tree!

About 15,000 types of plants also grow on Borneo. Some are carnivorous. They lure insects and small animals into a trap filled with liquid. Then they slowly digest their meal.

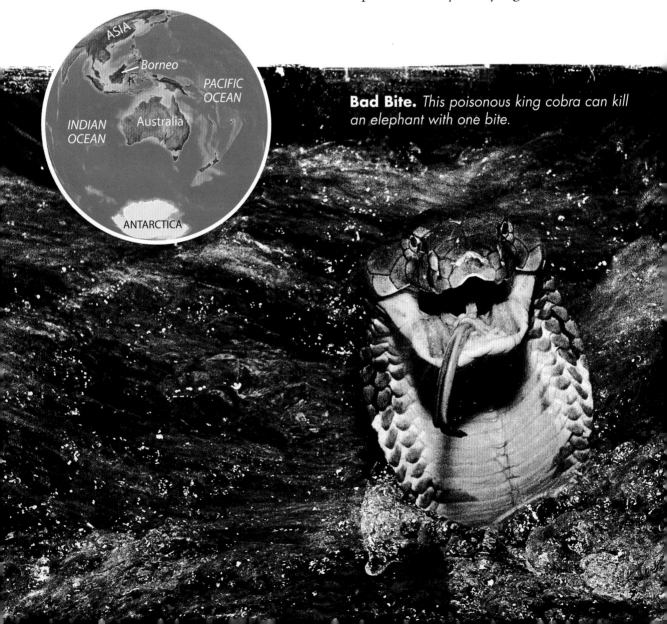

Bad Bite. *This poisonous king cobra can kill an elephant with one bite.*

Telling Borneo's Story

Every year, scientists find about 30 new plants and animals on Borneo. One recent find is a sticky-bellied catfish. Many creatures haven't even been named yet.

Klum takes a photo of a lizard with a growth shaped like a leaf on its nose. What kind of lizard is it? No one is sure. Borneo is a place where you can find things few people have ever seen before, Klum says.

The thrill draws Klum back to Borneo again and again. So far, he's traveled there more than 40 times. Once there, he goes to extremes to find and photograph Borneo's wildlife.

Klum dangles from hot-air balloons. He sits on branches 61 meters (200 feet) above the ground. He wades through waters infested with bloodsucking leeches.

Why? Klum wants to share the Borneo he loves. His pictures tell an amazing story.

Hungry Plant. *Low's pitcher plant eats insects, frogs, and even rats.*

Eye in the Sky. *To photograph the rain forest, Mattias Klum dangles from a hot-air balloon.*

Camera Shy. *Klum waded through mud and followed well-worn trails to find the shy bearded pig.*

Amazing Animals

Klum's quest takes him to many cool places in Borneo. One day, he canoes through a **mangrove** forest and calls out: "Eeow! Eeow! Eeow!" Voices call back: "Eeow, eeow!" They come from one of Borneo's rarest primates, the proboscis monkey.

Troops of proboscis monkeys can only be found living in the mangroves on Borneo. "Proboscis" means nose. The male monkeys have a seriously droopy nose. It hangs so low, it reaches the animal's chin. Females have daintier, pointy noses.

Both males and females have huge potbellies, and their stomachs are divided into sections. That helps them digest tough foods like mangrove leaves.

Klum spots a really strange creature standing near the water. It munches jellyfish and dead crabs. Long strands of wiry hair grow from its face. It's one of the female bearded pigs of Borneo. "This is hard to beat!" Klum thinks.

Flying lizard

Things That Fly

On another day, Klum climbs 46 meters (150 feet) up a rain forest tree. He carefully sits on a branch. A tent of nets and tarps camouflages him. From this perfect perch, he spots playful orangutans and colorful birds.

Mammals, frogs, snakes, and lizards soar through the trees, too. Borneo is home to more than 30 kinds of gliding animals. That's more than any other place on Earth. Once, a flying dragon lizard landed on Klum's head!

If he's lucky, he glimpses a paradise tree snake. It can travel 20 meters (60 feet) through the air from tree to tree. It flings itself from a branch, and then it flattens its body. It looks like a boomerang. "It just slithers through the air," Klum says.

Another flying creature looks like a kite made from a brown paper bag. It's the colugo. Billowy flaps of skin stretch from its jaw to its toes and the tip of its tail. The skin works like a parachute, keeping the colugo in the air. This mammal is called a "flying lemur," though it's not really a lemur at all.

Borneo's rain forest also is home to more traditional flyers. Klum spies jewel-colored birds flitting through the trees. The tiny Whitehead's trogon is a splash of scarlet and blue against green leaves.

On one trip, Klum sits in a tree and waits and waits. Three weeks later, he gets his shot. A turkey-sized bird lands and plucks a ripe fig. It's a rhinoceros hornbill, with a red and yellow horn-like growth jutting out above its beak.

Proboscis monkey

Tree Travelers. *Orangutans move through the trees.*

Surprise Attack. *Ready to strike prey, a Wagler's pit viper drapes itself over the branches.*

Vanishing Forests

The wild Borneo in Klum's photos is the place he fell in love with 20 years ago. That paradise still exists, but Borneo is changing.

When Klum returns to Borneo now and looks through his camera lens, it's what he doesn't see that upsets him. Where are all the trees? Borneo's forests are disappearing.

Klum takes photos of bulldozers and bare fields. He takes pictures of giant logs floating down muddy rivers. These new photos tell a different part of Borneo's story.

Loggers cut down trees to make furniture, paper, and more. Miners knock down trees to dig for gold, coal, and valuable minerals.

Farmers burn rain forests to plant rows of oil palm trees. Oil from the trees' fruit is used in cookies and potato chips. It's also in soaps and fuel. Growers call it "green gold" because they make a lot of money selling it.

The problem of **deforestation** began before Klum came to Borneo, but it's gotten much worse in the last 20 years.

Animals at Risk

Today, only about half of Borneo's forests remain. As a result, many of Borneo's plants and animals are endangered. The proboscis monkey is in trouble. So are the rhinoceros hornbill and the orangutan. Each one has fewer safe places to live.

It's harder for Klum to find certain animals. On earlier trips, he woke every morning to gibbons chattering outside his campsite. Now some mornings are quiet.

Gibbon

Saving Borneo

Still, there is hope for the future. Many people are working hard to save Borneo and its amazing wildlife. One big plan is called The Heart of Borneo. It's an agreement between the three countries on Borneo: Indonesia, Malaysia, and Brunei. It would **conserve** nearly a third of the island.

Loggers could take some, but not all, of the trees from this area. Vast sections would be protected, so they couldn't be turned into oil palm farms. That may help protect the area's plants and animals.

Soon Klum will head to Borneo again. What creatures will he find this time? He doesn't know yet.

He'll search for the increasingly hard-to-find orangutan. He may finally photograph an adult giant reticulated python, the longest snake in the world.

He hopes the animals' faces will make people care about Borneo. His photographs will keep telling the story of Borneo's present—and, hopefully, its future.

WORDWISE

biodiverse: having a great number of animal and plant species

conserve: keep from being wasted or lost

deforestation: when all the trees are removed

mangrove: tree that grows in marshy and coastal areas

Wanted Wood. *Loggers cut trees in Borneo's rain forest. Wood is used for furniture, houses, and even chopsticks.*

Shrinking Forest. *Large sections of the rain forest have been cut down to make way for oil palm farms and roads.*

BORNEO'S BOUNTY

More than 16,000 different kinds of animals and plants live on Borneo. What makes this island perfect for so many species? From mysterious mangroves to towering rain forests, Borneo has a variety of habitats. Many are in The Heart of Borneo (outlined in black). Meet Borneo's amazing wildlife.

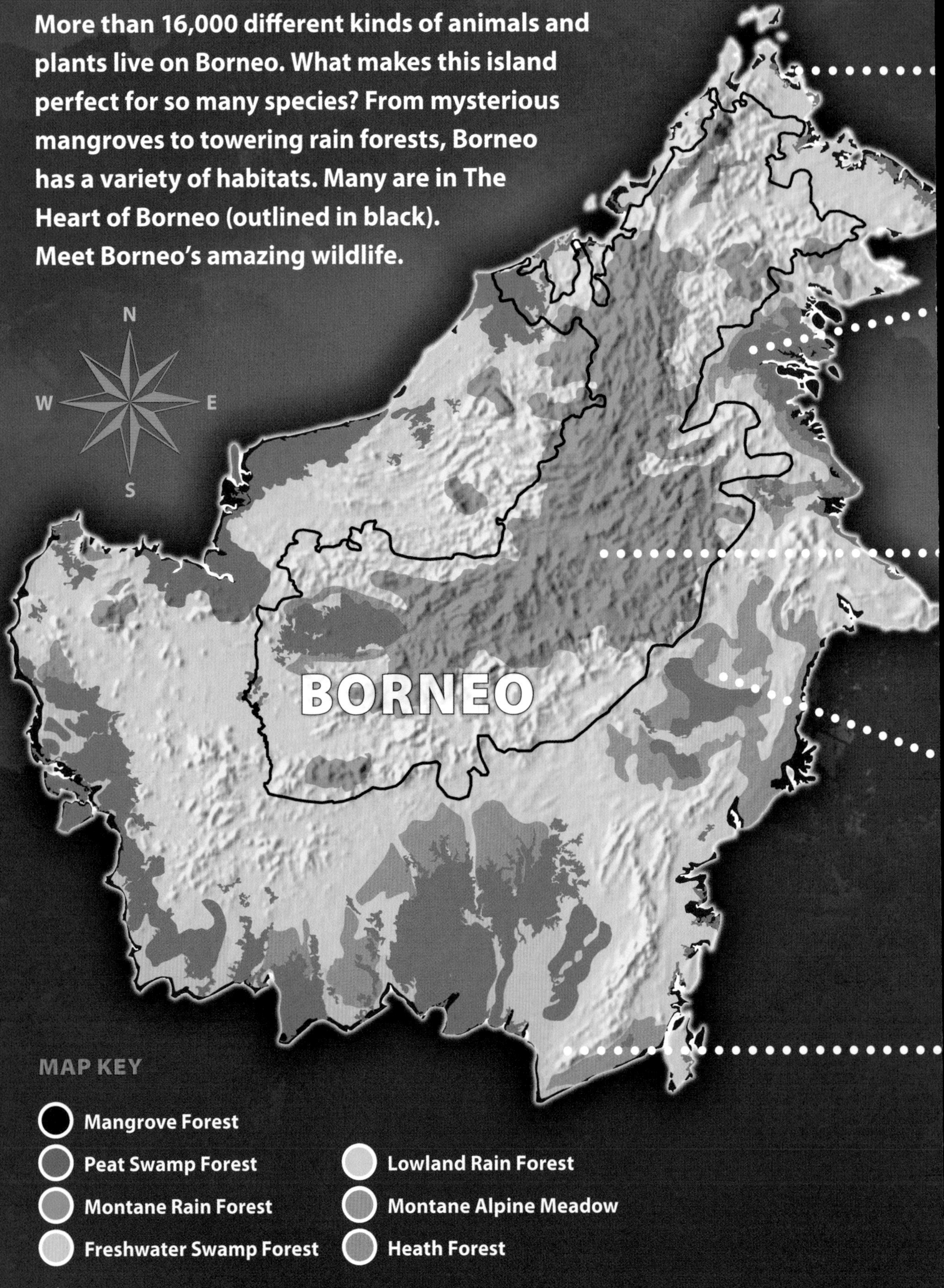

N
W   E
S

BORNEO

MAP KEY

- Mangrove Forest
- Peat Swamp Forest
- Montane Rain Forest
- Freshwater Swamp Forest
- Lowland Rain Forest
- Montane Alpine Meadow
- Heath Forest

Mangrove Forest

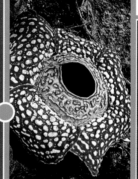

During the day, Wagler's pit vipers often lie coiled and motionless in the branches of mangrove trees. At night, these poisonous snakes hunt. Pits on their cheeks sense heat to help the vipers find prey.

Wagler's pit viper

Peat Swamp Forest

Orangutans live in peat swamp forests and other lowland habitats. These primates grip branches with strong hands and feet as they swing through the trees. They even hang upside down by their feet! Each night, they build sleeping nests in the trees.

Orangutans

Montane Rain Forest

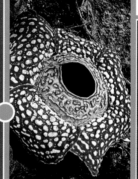

Some of the largest flowers in the world grow in Borneo's montane rain forest. Rafflesia smell and look like rotting meat. The smell attracts the flies that pollinate them so the plants can create new flowers.

Rafflesia

Freshwater Swamp Forest

Silvered leaf monkeys are arboreal, or live in trees. Troops of about 10 to 50 monkeys make their homes in trees that grow in such coastal habitats as freshwater swamps. The babies have orange fur. Their fur turns silver by the time the babies are five months old.

Silvered leaf monkeys

Lowland Rain Forest

Rhinoceros hornbills are the largest hornbill on Borneo. They feast on figs that grow in lowland rain forest trees. The female nests in a hollow tree. She goes inside the tree to lay her eggs and builds a wall to block the opening. The male feeds her through a tiny hole in the wall until the eggs hatch.

Rhinoceros hornbill

Call of the Wild

Do you hear the call of Borneo's really wild life? Answer these questions and find out.

1 Why is Mattias Klum so passionate about photographing Borneo's wildlife?

2 What makes it possible for so many different kinds of plants and animals to live in Borneo?

3 What do the people of Borneo need? What happens because of this?

4 Why is it difficult for Klum to find certain animals now?

5 Which plant or animal from Borneo would you like to know more about? Why?